T0373865

Official Cambridge Exam Preparation

FUN Skills

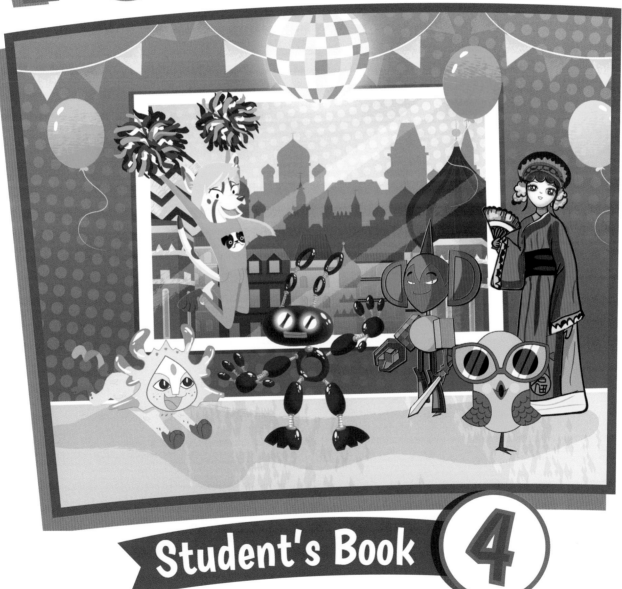

Student's Book

4

Bridget Kelly ● **David Valente**

Cambridge University Press
www.cambridge.org/elt

Cambridge Assessment English
www.cambridgeenglish.org

Information on this title: www.cambridge.org/9781108563673

© Cambridge University Press and Cambridge Assessment 2020

First published 2020

20 19 18 17 16 15 14 13 12 11 10 9 8

Printed in Poland by Opolgraf

A catalogue record for this publication is available from the British Library

ISBN 978-1-108-56367-3 Student's Book and Home Booklet with Online Activities

Contents

Map of the book

Unit	Topic	Skills focus	Can do	
1 **About me** page 6	Personal details	**Reading and Writing** Copy the correct names next to their descriptions	Read and understand simple descriptions of pictures and familiar topics	Song
2 **Routines** page 10	Regular activities	**Reading and Writing** Choose the correct answer to a question from three possible answers	Understand basic questions	Chant
		*Review Units 1–2 page 14*		
3 **All about town** page 16	Places around town	**Listening** Listen for words, names and detailed information Match words heard and pictures **Speaking** Talk about trips to places in town	Understand simple spoken descriptions Describe a regular activity	Chant
4 **Are you sporty?** page 20	Sports	**Speaking** Understand the beginning of a story Continue the story based on a series of pictures **Reading and Writing** Complete gaps in a text using words provided	Tell a very simple story with the help of pictures Complete sentences using the context to identify the correct word	
		*Review Units 3–4 page 24*		
5 **My dream school** page 26	School facilities	**Reading and Writing** Complete sentences Respond to questions Write sentences	Read and understand short texts about familiar topics with the help of pictures	Song Think Big
6 **Food around the world** page 30	International food	**Listening** Listen for words, colours and specific information Colour items according to instructions heard **Speaking** Suggest a picture that is different and explain why	Understand simple spoken descriptions Give simple spoken descriptions of objects, pictures and actions	Think Big
		*Review Units 5–6 page 34*		

① About me

Hi, my name is Lily. I'm 10 years old. I live with my grandparents in a village near a big national park in the jungle. I love watching the animals through the telescope on our balcony. I can see parrots in the trees and sometimes elephants.
I can also hear the birds and the waterfall at night when I'm in bed. My grandma says I'm very brave because I'm never scared of the animal sounds.

On Saturday afternoons, I go to the town centre with my grandpa. Our favourite places are the shopping centre and the roller disco. Roller skating is really, really, really fun! My grandpa is great at roller skating and his favourite drink is lychee milkshake. Lychees are his favourite fruit.

I don't have a pet, but a bat visits our balcony at night. I call him Charlie and he can hang upside down! Guess what Charlie likes to drink… Yes, that's right, lychee milkshake, the same as grandpa!

---

❶ **Meet Lily. Look at the pictures and read the questions below. Don't read the text yet. Guess the answers with a friend.**

1 How old is Lily? _____

2 Who does she live with? _____

3 What does she like doing at home? _____

4 What does she do at the weekends? _____

❷ 👁 **Now read Lily's description and check your guesses. Write your answers on the lines above.**

❸ **Check your answers with your friend.**

TIP!

How old? = circle the numbers.
Who? = circle names of family members.
What? = underline names of activities.

4 ✏️ **Lily wants to know about you! Write your answers below.**

1 Are you afraid of the dark? _____

2 What can you hear outside your window at night? _____

3 Can you buy lychees in your shops? _____

4 What is your favourite milkshake? _____

5 🎧 02 **Listen to the three children singing Lily's song. Say the words in your head.**

Hey Lily!

A: Hey Lily!

B: Hey you!

A: What can we do in Kota Kinabalu?

B: We can watch elephants through my telescope!

A: Is that true?

C: Hey Lily!

B: Hey you!

C: What can we do in Kota Kinabalu?

B: We can go shopping and roller skating too!

C: Is that true?

A: Hey Lily!

B: Hey you!

A: What can we do in Kota Kinabalu?

B: We can drink milkshakes with Charlie the bat!

A: Is that true?

ABC: Yes, it's true!!!

6 🎧 03 **Sing Lily's song in groups of three. Take turns to be A, B and C. Do the actions, click your fingers and be rappers!**

1 👁 **Look and read about Lily's friends from around the world. Choose the correct names and write them on the lines. There is one example.**

Emma

Michael

Katy

Holly

George

Sarah

Harry

David

This is me with my uncle on our farm. I love helping him with the animals!
Emma

2 This is me with my mum, dad and little brother. He's 6 years old. _____

4 This is me on my mum's back! And my sister is on my dad's back! We're playing games.
_____

1 I have no brothers or sisters. I'm watching TV with my parents on the sofa.
_____

3 This is me with my aunt. We're in the garden, and we really love flowers!
_____

5 I live with my grandparents, just like Lily! They are my favourite people!
_____

2 🖊 Talk about the two extra pictures with your friend.
Write about the two children.

_____

_____

3 💬 Ask and answer the questions with four friends.
Tell them two true things and two false things about you.
Write your friend's answers in the table.

Friend's **NAME**	What do you do at **HOME?**	What do you do at the **WEEKEND?**
1		
2		
3		
4		

4 Look at your friends' answers. What is true and what is false?
Tell the class all the funny false things about your friends.

② Routines

① 💬 **Look at all the pictures. Guess which pet belongs to who. Tell a friend.**

② 👁 **Read what the children say to check your guesses.**

Julia

Bruno is my pet parrot and he's a brilliant dancer! Every Sunday afternoon we go samba dancing. Every morning before school, Bruno and I practise our samba moves. We go to a big dance competition once a year. **What do you do before school?**

Chi

My pet lizard, Hong, really likes swimming. On Saturday mornings, we go to a huge pool near my house. There are lots of slides and diving boards. Hong is the best diver. **What do you do at weekends?**

Emma

Ramona is my pet rabbit and her favourite food is strawberry pancakes. Every morning for breakfast Ramona eats strawberry pancakes and is VERY fat! We have a picnic with my family on Sunday afternoons. Ramona always comes to our picnics and guess what she eats? STRAWBERRY PANCAKES! **What do you usually have for breakfast?**

Asim

My pet donkey, Azzizi, lives with my aunt and uncle, but I visit him every Friday afternoon. We sometimes go water skiing on the river and Azzizi is SO good at water skiing! In the evenings, we watch comedies on TV and laugh a lot! **What do you usually watch on TV?**

③ **Check your answers with your friend. Did you guess right?**

4 👁 **Read the sentences below and choose which is correct. Work with a friend. There is one example.**

TIP!

Read carefully – read slowly and check each fact.

Bruno
Ⓐ He is a great dancer.
B He is a terrible dancer.

1 Azzizi
A They go water skiing on Sundays.
B They go water skiing on Fridays.

2 Bruno
A He dances in a TV competition every year.
B He dances in a samba competition every year.

3 Ramona
A She eats a lot of pancakes.
B She doesn't eat any pancakes.

4 Hong
A She is scared of diving.
B She isn't scared of diving.

5 Bruno
A They usually practise their dances before school.
B They usually practise their dances after school.

6 Azzizi
A They watch funny shows on TV.
B They watch football games on TV.

5 💬 **Do a class survey. Talk to four friends. Write their names and ask questions about their routines. Make short notes.**

	Friend 1	Friend 2	Friend 3	Friend 4
What do you do before school?				
What do you do at weekends?				
What do you usually have for breakfast?				
What do you usually watch on TV?				
What do you do after school?				
What do you eat on your birthday?				

❶ 🖊 **Work with three friends. Write a chant about a dream pet and their amazing routines. Choose one word from each list. Think of a pet name with your friend. There is one example.**

Animals
dolphin
kangaroo
penguin
snail
shark
whale

Fun activities
ice skating
roller skating
skateboarding
playing in a band
texting friends
playing the piano

Places
funfair
farm
sports centre
swimming pool
supermarket
zoo

When
always
before school
after school
every day
every weekend

My pet _dolphin_ **is called** _Alfonso_ .
It loves _ice skating_ **at the** _sports centre_
after school . **My pet is so coooooooool!**

Our Amazing Pets Chant!

Me
My pet _____ is called _____ .
It loves _____
at the _____
_____ .
My pet is sooooo cool!

Name of friend: _____
My pet _____ is called _____ .
It loves _____
at the _____
_____ .
My pet is sooooo cool!

Name of friend: _____
My pet _____ is called _____ .
It loves _____
at the _____
_____ .
My pet is sooooo cool!

Name of friend: _____
My pet _____ is called _____ .
It loves _____
at the _____
_____ .
My pet is sooooo cool!

❷ 🔊 04 **Listen to the chant on page 66. Then practise the chant with your group. Click your fingers and keep the rhythm. Then, say your chant for your class.**

❸  **Read each question and circle the best answer. There is one example.**

Jim: What did you do on Sunday morning?
Fred: **A** I'll see you about 10 o'clock.
    Ⓑ I had pancakes at Grandma's.
    C I don't get up early.

1 Jim: Can you come to my house next weekend?
Fred: **A** Me too!
    B Great idea!
    C Well done!

2 Jim: What time can you come to my house?
Fred: **A** Yes, I can.
    B I enjoy travelling by train.
    C On Friday evening, I think.

3 Jim: Would you like to play my new computer game with me?
Fred: **A** Yes, you gave it to them.
    B No, this is the best one.
    C OK, let's do that.

4 Jim: When do you play computer games?
Fred: **A** Every day.
    B That's right.
    C Very carefully.

TIP!
Read the question twice.
Read A, B and C before you circle an answer.

❹ **Work with your friend. Ask and answer questions about imaginary pets from task 1.**

What is your pet's name?

What can your pet do?

Is your pet cool?

What is your pet?

❺ Tell your class who has an amazing pet!

Skills: Listening and Speaking

1 Talk to a friend about each picture. Write the words under the pictures.

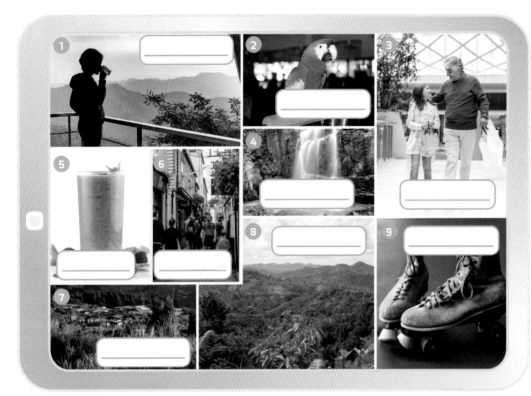

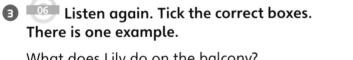

A parrot

B balcony

C waterfall

D jungle

E town centre

F roller skates

G milkshake

H village

I shopping centre

Mark: ___ / 10

2 〔05〕 **Listen. Who is talking? Say why!**

Lily's grandpa   Charlie the bat

3 〔06〕 **Listen again. Tick the correct boxes. There is one example.**

What does Lily do on the balcony?

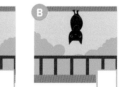

A   B   C ✓

1 What do they do on Saturdays?

A   B   C

2 Where do Lily and her grandpa go on Saturdays?

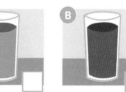

A   B   C

3 What milkshake does Lily's grandpa like best?

A   B   C

4 What does Charlie do on the balcony?

A   B   C

Mark: ___ / 4

Total: ___ / 14

Skills: Listening and Speaking

1 `07` Who is speaking? Is it Asim, Julia, Chi or Emma? Listen and circle A, B, C or D. After you listen, check with a friend.

A    B    C    D

Mark: ___ / 1

2 `08` Listen again and write in the calendar. After you listen, check with your friend. There is one example.

	Fridays	Saturdays
mornings	1 *take the bus*	4
afternoons	2	5
evenings	3	6

Mark: ___ / 5

3 Complete YOUR weekend calendar. Write the names of your weekend days. Then write your routine.

My Weekend

mornings	1	4
afternoons	2	5
evenings	3	6

Mark: ___ / 6

4 Ask your friend about their weekend routine. Write their answers in the orange calendar.

My Buddy's Weekend

mornings	1	4
afternoons	2	5
evenings	3	6

Mark: ___ / 6

5 Who has the best weekend?

Mark: ___ / 2

Total: ___ ___ / 20

3 All about town

pet shop

lake

park

① 👁 **Look at the map and label the places with the correct words.**

> supermarket   library   sports centre   funfair   cinema
> market square   train station   hospital

② `09` **Where did they go? Draw lines on the map. Use a red pencil for Kim and a blue pencil for Ben. Listen and check.**

Kim: I parked in the car park in my small, red car,
Then I went to the hospital to see my sick grandma
Then I bought a bag of apples in the market square
And last of all I met my friends at the big funfair!

Ben: I arrived at the station on a new orange train
Then I went to the cinema to watch a film called *Rain*.
Then I went to the New Café to drink a cup of tea.
And last of all I read some comics in the library.

③ 💬 **Now say the chant yourselves.**

4 Which words have sounds that rhyme? Draw lines.

1 car   grandma

2 square   funfair

3 train   rain

4 tea   library

5 Look at the pictures, choose places on the map on page 16 and write the third verse for the chant in task 2. Try to use sounds that rhyme at the ends of the sentences.

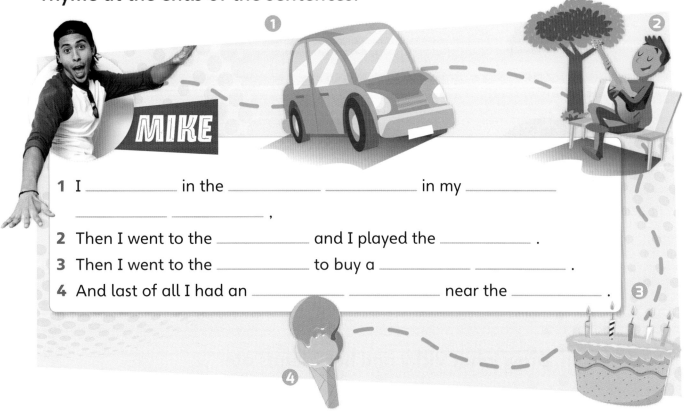

1 I _____ in the _____ _____ in my _____
   _____ _____ ,
2 Then I went to the _____ and I played the _____ .
3 Then I went to the _____ to buy a _____ _____ .
4 And last of all I had an _____ near the _____ .

6 Now think of some places in town and write a verse about you. Try to make it rhyme.

I _____ .
Then I _____ .
Then I _____ .
And last of all I _____ .

1 🔟 **Which places did each person go to? Write names next to the places.**

TIP!
You will hear about the people in a different order to the photos on the page.

bookshop _____	market _____ *Vicky* _____
library _____	shopping centre _____
park _____	sports centre _____
pet shop _____	supermarket _____

Zoe   Dan   Tom

Vicky ☐f   Peter   Eva

2 1️⃣1️⃣ **Listen. Draw what Vicky and her friends ate.**

❸ 💬 Look at the pictures below. Where can you buy each thing?

❹ 🔊 12 Listen. Write the letters by the person in task 1 who bought each item. There is one example.

Ⓐ

Ⓑ

Ⓒ

Ⓓ

Ⓔ

Ⓕ

❺ Write the names of two places on a piece of paper. Talk to your friend about when you go to those places.

I go to the lake to fly my kite after school.

4 Are you sporty?

4 i __ e
s __ __ ti __ g

5 __ o __ __ e r
s k __ __ i __ g

3 b __ __ __ __ b __ ll

1 f __ __ t __ a __ __

7 d *a* n *c* e

2 __ __ s k __ t b a __ __

6 s __ i l i __ __

❶ ✏️ **Look and complete the names of the activities. There is one example.**

❷ 🔊 13 **Listen. Complete the sentences with the verbs in the correct form. You can use some verbs more than once.**

do   score   move   jump   kick   throw   hit   swim   catch

1   Daisy's good at _____ in skates. She isn't good at _____ , kicking or throwing a ball.

2   Mary's good at _____ . She isn't good at _____ .

3   Charlie's good at music. He isn't good at _____ a ball.

4   Julia's good at _____ and _____ and _____ balls. She isn't good at _____ the ball.

5   Jack's good at _____ in skates. He isn't good at _____ .

6   Fred isn't good at music. He's good at _____ balls with a bat.

7   Vicky isn't good at _____ sports with a bat and ball. She's good at _____ balls and _____ goals.

❸ 👁 **Are you sporty? Ask a friend and circle the answers. Count their answers.**

1 What do you enjoy doing most?
   A playing tennis B walking C playing video games
2 How often do you do sport?
   A every day B one or two days a week C never
3 What do you enjoy doing most?
   A doing sport B watching sport C reading a book
4 Which one are you really good at?
   A running quickly B running slowly C sitting down

2–3 As: You're really sporty. You love moving and you don't like sitting down all day.

2–3 Bs: You're a little sporty, but you don't want to do sport all the time.

2–3 Cs: You're not sporty at all. You really like using computers and reading books.

❹ **Read about Jane and circle the best words.**

Jane is **really sporty / a little sporty / not sporty at all.**

Jane's Blog

I enjoy doing sport, but I only do it one or two days a week. I'm good at running and jumping, so I like playing basketball. I'm not good at hitting a ball with a bat, so I don't like playing baseball. I enjoy watching sport on TV and I really like walking in the countryside.

❺ ✏ **Now write four sentences about you. What sports do you like / not like? What sports are / aren't you good at?**

❶ 🔊 14 **Look at picture 1. Listen and write T (true) or F (false).**

1 Alice and Luis are brother and sister. _____

2 It's a beautiful morning. _____

3 They are sailing on the sea. _____

A picnic on the lake

 ❷ 💬 **Work with your friend. Tell the story for pictures 2, 3 and 4.**

❸ Read this dialogue. Which picture is it?

Alice: Here you are! You can have my sandwich.

Luis: Thanks, Alice!

❹ ✏️ **Write a short dialogue for one of the pictures.**

❺ 💬 **Read your dialogue to a friend. Which picture is it?**

❻ What sports do the photos show?

1 _____

2 _____

3 _____

4 _____

❼ 👁 ✏ Read the text. Choose the right words and write them on the lines.

near   these   making   ~~in~~   have   cleverest

Sheep live ____*in*____ many countries in the world. There are many kinds of sheep. Most sheep are white, but some are white with black faces and some 1 _____ black faces and bodies.

Sheep live in fields 2 _____ farms or in the mountains. They are good at walking up mountains. They like grass and eat a lot of it every day. Farmers get milk from 3 _____ animals and in some places, people like 4 _____ cheese from this milk. Sheep also give us meat.

Some people say that sheep aren't the 5 _____ animals in the world, but I don't think this is correct. What do you think?

Review Unit 3

Skills: Reading and Speaking

1 Read about Fred's day in town and number the places in order.

1

First, I took the bus to a very big shop that sells lots of different things like food, toys and sometimes clothes. I bought a birthday cake there to give to my sister. Second, I walked to one of my favourite places to read a book. I like it because it's very quiet. The next place I went wasn't quiet at all! There were lots of people there having fun! I went on some exciting rides and I had an ice cream.

After that, I walked to the big square in the centre of town to buy some fruit. Farmers sell food there every day. Then I went for a swim and played table tennis with my friends. There's a great place where you can do that near the train station. In the evening, I saw my sister Amy because it was her birthday. We watched a film and ate birthday cake. It was a fun day!

Mark: ___ / 6

2 Choose a place and say what you did there. Can your partner guess the place?

pet shop   station   hospital   shopping centre   café

Mark: ___ / 6

Total: ___ ___ / 12

I went there to buy a puppy.   Was it the pet shop?

Skills: Listening and Writing

1 🔊 15 **Listen and draw lines from Sofia to the things she needs.**

Mark: ___ / 4

2 **Plan a sports holiday and write a list.**

My sports holiday

Day / time	sport	What to take
Monday afternoon	football	

Mark: ___ / 8
Total: ___ / 12

CHECKLIST

I used capital letters for the days of the week. ☐

I checked my spelling. ☐

My handwriting is clear. ☐

(5) My dream school

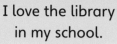

I love the library in my school.

FILIP, Poland

We are lucky – we have a swimming pool at my school!

ASYA, Turkey

ANDRES, Mexico

We have big windows in my class. They are great.

We have 10 new computers at my school.

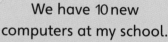

KANYA, Thailand

1 💬 **Meet four more new friends. Which school would you like to visit? Talk to your friend.**

2 ✏️ **Four dream schools! Finish the sentences and answer the questions.**

Asya

Asya's dream school is in a _cinema_ .

What's the teacher wearing? Superhero _clothes_ .

Filip

1 Filip's dream school is in the _____ .

2 Where's the classroom? _____ .

Andres

3 Andres' dream school is in a _____ .

4 What are they drinking? _____ .

Kanya

5 Kanya's dream school is in a _____ .

6 What are they reading? _____ .

3 👁 **Read about the children's dream schools. Write A, B, C or D.**

A Asya   B Filip   c Andres   D Kanya

1 In my dream school, the older children teach us English. Our classroom is in a fantastic café and we wear baseball caps. We sometimes play speaking games in our English lessons and drink purple milkshakes. YUM! _____

2 My dream school is in a big circus and our teachers are clowns. We laugh a lot because we read English comics and sing songs. Everyone wears funny circus clothes. GREAT! _____

3 My dream school is brilliant! We have English lessons in a cinema. We wear superhero clothes and read e-books! My dream school is exciting because my teachers are superheroes. My English lessons are always FUN! _____

4 My dream school is the best! Our English lessons are in the jungle and the classrooms are in tree houses. We wear pirate clothes and my English teacher is a pirate too! The lessons are never boring. WOW! _____

4 **Read about the children's dream schools again. Work with your friend and write in the table.**

TIP!
Underline the answers in the bubbles. Copy the spellings correctly!

Our dream school!

Name	Where is the classroom?	Who are the teachers?	What do the children wear?
Filip	in a tree house	pirates	pirate clothes
Andres	1 _____	2 _____	3 _____
Kanya	4 _____	5 _____	6 _____
Asya	7 _____	8 _____	9 _____

5 💬 **Which dream school do you like best? Why? Tell your friend!**

1 🚇 16 **Listen to the song. Write the missing words with your friend. There are two examples.**

My dream school is really ___brilliant___!
Our classroom is in a ___cinema___.
We use e-books to learn English.
It's like you are on Mars!!

Asya

My dream school is in the **1** _____. There's always lots to see and do. We are **2** _____ who look for **3** _____. Our classroom really is the best.

Filip

My dream school is so fantastic! Our classroom is in a cool **4** _____. We drink **5** _____ and wear **6** _____ _____. Visit my dream school today.

Andres

My dream school is like a wonderland. Our teachers here are all great **7** _____. We read comics and we sing **8** _____ songs. Come inside and have a look around my dream **9** _____.

Kanya

2 🚇 17 **Listen to the song again and check your answers.**

3 ✏️ **Write about your dream school! Choose ONE word from each list.**

My dream school!

1 My dream school is in _____.
2 The teachers in my dream school are _____.
3 We wear _____ in my dream school.

1 Classrooms   space   a playground   a funfair

2 Teachers   aliens   robots   monsters

3 Clothes   space clothes   sports clothes   jeans and T-shirts

4 💬 **Use your answers from task 3. Ask your friends if anyone has the same dream school.**

> Where are the classrooms in your dream school?

> Who are the teachers in your dream school?

> What do you wear in your dream school?

5 **Tell the class about your dream schools!**

THINK **BIG**

Think about the rest of your dream school! Then read the questions and write the answers with a friend.

1 What do you do in your English lessons?

2 What special things are in the school building?

3 What is most fun about your dream school?

6 Food around the world

My favourite food is noodles with chicken.

We have great pasta and fantastic pizza.

Chanchai, Thailand.

Jenny, USA.

We have delicious burgers and fries.

Stefano, Italy.

Sebastian, Mexico.

We love fresh fish, we don't cook it!

6 Matiana, Peru.

We have lots of fresh fruit like mangoes.

My family love a typical dinner of fish cooked in fruit juice.

Ayako, Japan.

❶ Read and match the countries with the foods.

1 Japan   2 Mexico   3 Thailand   4 Italy   5 USA   6 Peru

A pizza   B fresh fruit   C fish in fruit juice   D fresh fish

E burgers   F noodles

❷ 18 Listen and colour the food.

3 💬 Which is your favourite food? Write the numbers: 1–6. 1 = your favourite.

4 Compare with a friend.

> My favourite is noodles because I eat them with lots of cheese.

> My least favourite is…

fish sushi _____
fresh fruit _____
noodles _____
pizza _____
burgers _____
fish in fruit juice _____

5 👁 Look at the picture. Match the food words from basket A with the words in basket B. There is one example.

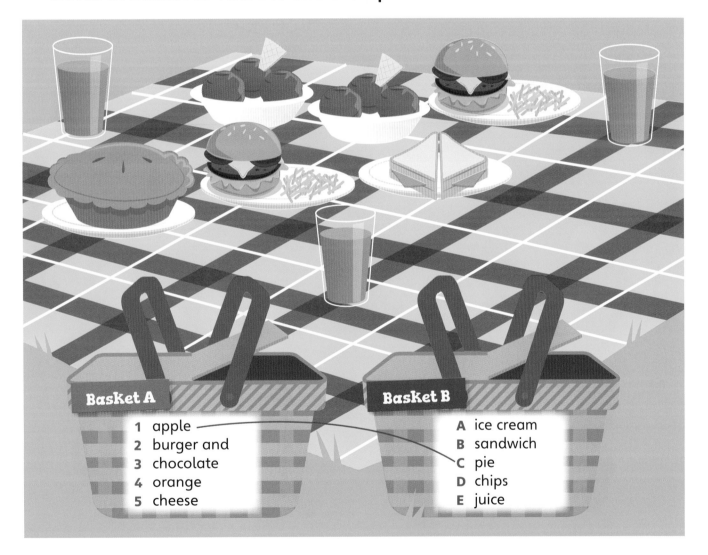

Basket A
1 apple
2 burger and
3 chocolate
4 orange
5 cheese

Basket B
A ice cream
B sandwich
C pie
D chips
E juice

6 🔊 19 Listen and point to the food.

7 🔊 20 Listen to the children again. In your group, take turns to dance when you hear the food you like.

I think the third one is different because it's a drink and the cake, fruit and biscuits are food. You eat them!

1 💬 **Look at the photos. Tell a friend which one is different. There is one example.**

2 ✏️ Choose words from the picnic baskets to make crazy combinations! Write five questions in the table.

		friend 1	friend 2	friend 3	friend 4
beans	onions				
honey	peas				
coconut	pineapple				
ice cream	coffee				
pasta	cake				
pancakes	chips				
salad	rice				
meatballs	noodles				

1 Do you like _____ on your _____ ? ☐ ☐ ☐ ☐
2 Do you like _____ on your _____ ? ☐ ☐ ☐ ☐
3 Do you like _____ on your _____ ? ☐ ☐ ☐ ☐
4 Do you like _____ on your _____ ? ☐ ☐ ☐ ☐
5 Do you like _____ on your _____ ? ☐ ☐ ☐ ☐

3 💬 Walk around the classroom and interview four friends. Put a tick (✓) for *Yes* and a cross (✗) for *No*. Answer their questions.

Do you like ice cream on your meatballs?   Yes, I do!   No, I don't!

4 Then tell your class who likes the best crazy combinations.

THINK BIG

Think about food from around the world. Answer the questions with a friend.

1 What food from other countries do you like?
2 What food from other countries can you find in your town / city?

Skills: Listening and Speaking

1 🔊 **21** **Listen to Masha from Russia and Chang from China. Circle the answers to the questions.**

MASHA

1 Where is Masha's dream school?

A    B    C

2 What does she wear?

A    B    C

3 Who are her teachers?

A   B   C

CHANG

1 Where is Chang's dream school?

A    B    C

2 Who are his teachers?

A    B    C

3 What does he wear?

A    B    C

Mark: ___ / 6

2 **Talk to four friends. Ask and answer the questions.**

1 Do you like Chang's or Masha's dream school best? Why?

2 Do you like your school? Why or why not?

3 What do you wear at school?

4 Who is your dream teacher? Why?

Mark: ___ / 4

Total: ___ / 10

Skills: Reading and Speaking

1 **Read about Masha, Chang and Yigit and colour their foods.**

What's your favourite food, Masha?

MASHA, Russia

I really love beetroot soup. It is famous in Russia. Beetroot is a red vegetable and the soup is red too. My dad cooks the best beetroot soup with orange carrots, white onions, yellow potatoes and brown sausage. I am hungry now!

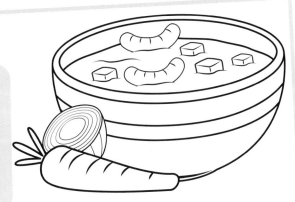

What do you often eat at home, Chang?

CHANG, China

My family likes to eat Chinese food called dim sum. My aunt and I make chicken feet dim sum. They are an orange colour and are my favourite! We often eat dim sum with red rice and green vegetables called bok choy at home.

What do Turkish children like to eat at parties, Yigit?

YIGIT, Turkey

My classmates and I go to the café near my school for birthday parties. They have the best meatballs and chips in my town! The meatballs are brown and the chips are yellow. We eat them with red tomatoes and white rice.

Mark: ___ / 12

2 **Talk to four friends. Ask and answer the questions.**

1 Whose food do you want to try? Masha's, Chang's or Yigit's? Why?

2 What's your favourite food from other countries?

3 What do you often eat at home?

4 What do you like to eat at parties?

Mark: ___ / 4

Total: ___ / 16

7 Sunny or cloudy?

WEATHER DIARY — MOSCOW, RUSSIA

Monday: Today the weather was very cold. There were clouds in the morning and there was snow in the afternoon. The snow was beautiful.

Sasha Petrov

HOT ☐ COLD ☐

WEATHER DIARY — CAIRO, EGYPT

Monday: The weather was hot and sunny today! But in the evening it was very windy and we had to stay inside.

Karim Masry

HOT ☐ COLD ☐

1 👁 **Look at the weather diaries. Tick (✓) the correct icons.**

2 **Write the missing nouns and adjectives.**

Weather nouns

| | rain | | snow | | cloud |

weather adjectives

| sunny | | windy | | icy | |

36

❸ **Look at the pictures in task 4 and write the number and letter. There is one example.**

rain _2A_   1 cloud _____   2 rainbow _____

3 snow _____   4 ice _____   5 wind _____   6 sun _____

❹ 🔊22 **Look, listen and tick (✓) the box. There is one example.**

1 Which T-shirt is Tom's?   A ☐   B ☐   C ✓

2 What was the weather like on Tuesday?   A ☐   B ☐   C ☐

3 What is the weather like now?   A ☐   B ☐   C ☐

4 What would Sarah like to do today?   A ☐   B ☐   C ☐

❺ 👁 **Choose words from task 2 to complete the sentences.**

1 There was a lot of _____ today. Now everything is white.

2 It was grey and _____ all morning, but it didn't rain.

3 It was very _____ , so we flew our kite.

4 The _____ was very hot today, so I stayed inside.

❻ ✏ **Make a weather diary for this week.**

❶ 🔊 **23** **Read and listen to the text.**

Clouds

What are clouds?

Watching clouds is fun, but did you know this? They have lots of very small drops of water in them? When it's very cold, clouds can have small drops of ice or snow in them, too.

When there aren't many clouds in the sky, the weather is often sunny and dry.

When there are a lot of clouds in the sky, the weather is often wet. Grey clouds have a lot more drops of water, ice or snow in them than white clouds.

Did you know there are ten different kinds of clouds? **Here are three of them.**

A **Cirrostratus** are thin, long clouds. You often see them before it snows.

B **Altostratus** are big, grey clouds. There are often lots of them on wet, rainy days.

C **Cumulus** are white clouds and they can be lots of different shapes. You often see them on hot, sunny days.

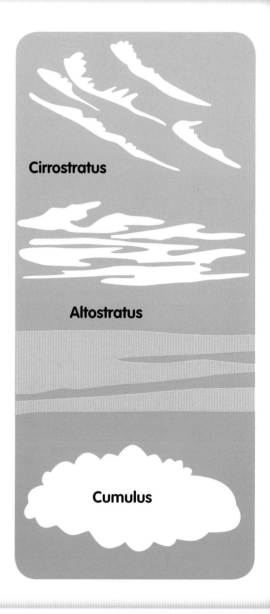

Cirrostratus

Altostratus

Cumulus

❷ 👁 **Read again and answer the questions.**

1   Why are some clouds grey?

_____ .

2   It's a hot sunny day. What kind of clouds can you see? _____ .

3   It's a rainy day and there isn't any sun. What kind of clouds can you see?

_____ .

4   There's a big white cloud in the sky. It's the shape of a rabbit.
    What kind of cloud is it? _____ .

5   What kinds of clouds can be very thin? _____ .

❸ Look outside. Then answer the questions.

What's the weather like today?
_____

Are there any clouds in the sky today?

Yes ☐   No ☐

Draw the clouds that you can see. Do you know what they are called?

That's OK! Draw a picture of the weather today.

❹ 💬 Look at the words and fill in the gaps about you. Then ask a friend.

Me	My friend
1 When it's rainy, I often _____ _____ _____ .	1 When it's rainy _____ often _____ .
2 When it's sunny, I often _____ _____ _____ .	2 When it's sunny, _____ often _____ .
3 When it's windy, I often _____ _____ _____ .	3 When it's windy, _____ often _____ .
4 The last time I saw snow was _____ _____ .	4 The last time _____ saw snow was _____ .
5 The last time I saw a rainbow was _____ _____ .	5 The last time _____ saw a rainbow was _____ _____ .
6 I like _____ weather the best.	6 _____ like _____ weather the best.

What do you do when it's ...?

When was the last time you saw ...?

What weather do you like best?

When it's rainy, I often watch DVDs.

The last time ...

I like ...

8 Last week

Monday

Zoe

A B C D E F G

❶ Look at the photos. What did Zoe do last week?

❷ **24** Now listen and write the days of the week. There is one example.

Monday Tuesday Wednesday Thursday
Friday Saturday Sunday

❸ **25** Listen again and write T (true) or F (false).

1   Zoe had pasta for lunch on Monday.   F
2   Zoe didn't like the film called 'Lizard'.
3   Zoe saw her grandma on Wednesday.
4   Zoe's uncle has a horse.
5   Zoe planted a tree at her school on Friday.
6   Zoe never goes shopping on Saturdays.
7   Zoe went to bed before 8 o'clock on Sunday.

❹ **26** Listen. Does the
voice go up or down?

Did you do your homework last week?   Yes, I did.

5 👁 **What did Fred do last weekend?**
Colour green for yes and red for no.

Fred

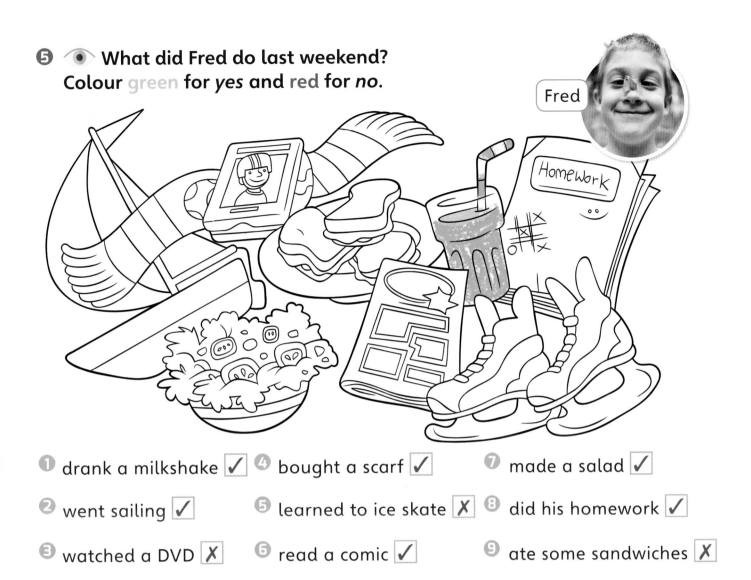

1 drank a milkshake ✓
2 went sailing ✓
3 watched a DVD ✗

4 bought a scarf ✓
5 learned to ice skate ✗
6 read a comic ✓

7 made a salad ✓
8 did his homework ✓
9 ate some sandwiches ✗

6 ✏ **Write four things you did last weekend.**

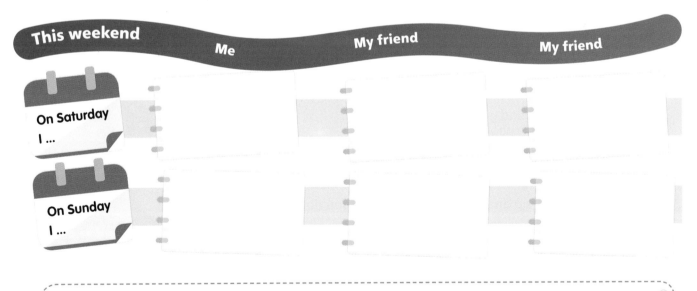

This weekend	Me	My friend	My friend
On Saturday I ...			
On Sunday I ...			

7 💬 **Ask your friends and write in the boxes in task 6.**

What did you do last weekend?

On Saturday, I went to the cinema and I made pancakes. On Sunday, I ...

❶ 👁 **Read the quiz. What do you think 'adventurous' means?**

❷ **Do the quiz with a friend.**

Quiz time!

Do you like to try new things?
How adventurous are you?
Do the quiz and find out.

You're in the park and you see an elephant. What do you do?

Make friends – elephants are cool!

1. **You're in the park and you see an elephant. What do you do?**
   a Make friends – elephants are cool!
   b Run away and hide! Elephants are scary!

2. **You're in a café and there are chocolate and cheese sandwiches for lunch. Do you try them?**
   a Yes, why not?
   b Ugh, never!

3. **Your friend invites you to go roller skating, but you don't know how to roller skate. Do you go?**
   a Yes, I can learn.
   b No, thanks – I think it's dangerous.

4. **It's very cold and it's snowing. Do you go outside, or stay inside?**
   a Go outside and play in the snow! It's fun!
   b Stay inside and watch DVDs. It's too cold!

5. **Your friend lives in a circus and invites you to be a clown one night. Do you do it?**
   a Yes, I love making people laugh.
   b No, thanks. I have to do my homework.

6. **You're walking in the countryside and you see a mountain in front of you. What do you do?**
   a Climb the mountain. It's exciting.
   b Go home. I'm tired!

7. **You're at the beach and you see an alien. It asks you to help it. What do you do?**
   a Ask the alien what it wants.
   b Run away and hide. Aliens are scary!

8. **One day you wake up and you can fly. What do you do?**
   a Fly around the world. It's brilliant!
   b Go to the doctor. I don't want to fly.

❸ 💬 **Talk with your friend. Do you think your friend is adventurous? Why? / Why not?**

I think you're adventurous because you want to make friends with an elephant ...

Mostly As - You're adventurous!

Mostly Bs - You're not very adventurous.

4 👁 **Read the story about an adventure. Which quiz question does it match?**

Last Saturday, I went to the beach. It was very sunny and I wanted to go for a swim. When I got there, I saw a green and purple alien on the beach.

'My name's Tub,' said the alien. 'I can't find my space-car. Can you help me? It's green!'

'Yes, I can help you,' I said.

So we looked for Tub's space-car on the beach.

'I can see it,' I said. 'It's under the sand!'

'Thanks!' said Tub. 'Now I can go home!'

Tub said goodbye and got in the space-car. Then Tub drove up into the sky. Look – here's a photo I took!

5 **Read the questions. Then read the story again and underline the answers with the correct colours.**

1 When did it happen? Where did it happen?

2 What was the weather like? Why did you go there?

3 Who / What did you see? What did they say? What did you say?

4 What did you do? Then what happened?

5 How did it end?

6 ✏ **Choose a question from the quiz and plan a story for it. Use the colours to make your plan.**

1 *Last* _____ / _____

2 *It was* _____ *and I* _____

3 _____ _____ _____

4 _____ _____

5 _____

7 **Now write your story and draw a picture.**

Review Unit 7

Skills: Writing and Speaking

1 Look and write what the weather was like last weekend. Use these words to help you. There is one example.

> rainbow   cloudy   snowed   windy   rained   sunny

1 Saturday morning

2 Saturday afternoon

3 Sunday morning

4 Sunday afternoon

1 *On Saturday morning it rained and it was cloudy.*

2 _____

3 _____

4 _____

Mark: ___ / 6

2 What did Anna do last weekend? Now write four sentences to tell the story. There is one example.

1 *On Saturday morning it rained and Anna rode her bike.*

2 _____

3 _____

4 _____

Mark: ___ / 6

3 Talk about the weather last weekend with your partner.

> What was the weather like on Saturday morning?

> On Saturday morning it was ...

> What was the weather like on Saturday afternoon?

Mark: ___ / 2

Total: ___ ___ / 14

Skills: Reading and Listening

1 **What did Ben's friends do last weekend? Read and write the names under the pictures.**

1

2

3

Hi, I'm Ben. I got a new camera for my birthday and last weekend I went out and took photos of some of my friends. I went to see Amy on Saturday morning. She likes exciting sports and she took me sailing. I didn't really enjoy it because I got sick.

4

5

I went to see my friend Alex in the afternoon. In this photo, he's making a milkshake for us. He made us dinner, too. He's really good at cooking.

Ben

My friend Sam isn't very adventurous. Last Sunday he read comics about aliens all day. I saw him in the morning and I took this photo of him.

Mark: ___ / 4

Look – here's a photo of Reem. She's learning how to be a clown. I went to the circus last Sunday afternoon to watch her. She's really funny! What did you and your friends do last weekend?

2 **27** **Listen to Ben. What's different? Make notes and then draw new photos for Amy, Alex, Sam and Reem.**

1 Amy

2 Alex

3 Sam

4 Reem

Mark: ___ / 8

Total: ___ ___ / 12

9 Jobs

1 💬 **Look at the picture and guess the jobs. Talk to a friend.**

Ben Emma Paul

Peter Daisy Zoe

2 28 **Listen and draw lines. There is one example.**

TIP!
Listen to ALL the conversation before you match.

❸ Number the jobs:
1 = My favourite job;
6 = I don't want to do this job.

❹ Talk with a friend. Say why you chose number 1 and number 6.

> I want to be a teacher because I love speaking English.

> I don't want to be a doctor because I don't like hospitals.

A teacher _____ ☐
B dentist _____ ☐
C film star _____ ☐
D nurse _____ ☐
E pop star _____ ☐
F doctor _____ ☐

❺ ✏️ Read Annie's post. Write a post about your favourite job.

Annie	Me

← → 🌐 ★

I want to be a cook because I love watching cooking on TV and my dad is a good cook too!

Annie	Me

← → 🌐 ★

I want to be _____ because _____ and _____ .

TIP!
Check your friend's post. Is the handwriting clear? Is the spelling correct? Do you understand the reasons?

1 👁 **Read and match. There is one example.**

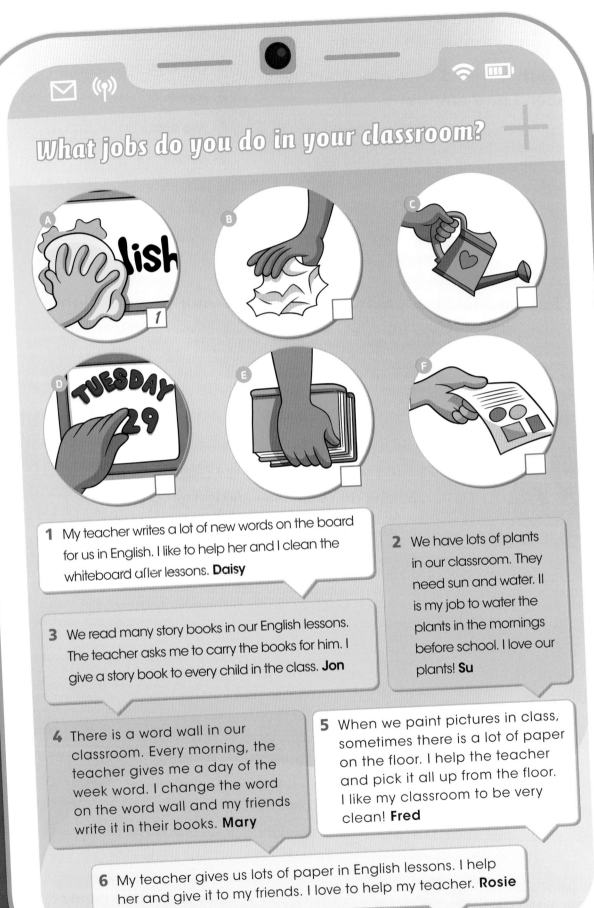

What jobs do you do in your classroom?

A

B

C

D — TUESDAY 29

E

F

1 My teacher writes a lot of new words on the board for us in English. I like to help her and I clean the whiteboard after lessons. **Daisy**

2 We have lots of plants in our classroom. They need sun and water. It is my job to water the plants in the mornings before school. I love our plants! **Su**

3 We read many story books in our English lessons. The teacher asks me to carry the books for him. I give a story book to every child in the class. **Jon**

4 There is a word wall in our classroom. Every morning, the teacher gives me a day of the week word. I change the word on the word wall and my friends write it in their books. **Mary**

5 When we paint pictures in class, sometimes there is a lot of paper on the floor. I help the teacher and pick it all up from the floor. I like my classroom to be very clean! **Fred**

6 My teacher gives us lots of paper in English lessons. I help her and give it to my friends. I love to help my teacher. **Rosie**

② 💬 **Work with a friend. Match the words to make classroom jobs.**

1 close
2 pick up
3 give out
4 put
5 clean
6 water

A the plants
B the windows
C the board
D the paper
E the books in the cupboard
F the story books

❸ **Walk around the classroom and interview four friends. Put a tick (✓) for *Yes* and a cross (✗) for *No*.**

In your classroom	Friend 1	Friend 2	Friend 3	Friend 4
1 Do you water the plants?				
2 Do you carry books for your teacher?				
3 Do you give out the paper and pencils?				
4 Do you put things in the cupboard?				
5 Do you clean the board?				
6 Do you pick up paper?				

❹ **After you finish, tell your class who helps the most in the classroom.**

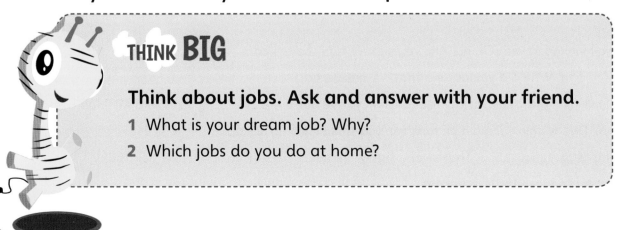

THINK BIG

Think about jobs. Ask and answer with your friend.
1 What is your dream job? Why?
2 Which jobs do you do at home?

10 At the hospital

1 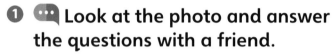 **Look at the photo and answer the questions with a friend.**

1 Who are the four people?

2 Where are they?

2 **Read Peter's story. Then talk with a friend. Is it a happy or a sad story?**

TIP!

First read quickly. You don't need to understand every word.

Yesterday was my birthday and my parents gave me some new paints as a ___present___ .
They know I love making pictures. I **1** _____ the paints on the school bus and used
them to make a picture for my **2** _____ , Mr Hall. I used nearly all the colours and did
a picture of some **3** _____ in the jungle because they're his favourite birds.

At school, Mr Hall was inside our classroom. 'Good morning, Mr Hall,' I said. 'I have something
for you!'

Mr Hall looked at me. 'Oh no! Are you sick, Peter?' he asked.

'No, I'm fine. Why did you ask me that?' I answered.

'You look terrible. Your face is red. I think you've got a **4** _____ ,' said Mr Hall.

'Ha ha. This is paint! I did a picture for you this morning,' I said.

Mr Hall **5** _____ .'That's very funny,' he said. 'Lots of children are sick today.
I'm happy to learn that you're not.'

❸ 👁 ✏️ **Read Peter's story again. Choose a word from 3. Write the correct word next to numbers 1–5 in task 2. There is one example.**

present

temperature

pointed

laughed

pandas

teacher

doctor

opened

parrots

❹ **Choose the best name for the story. Tell your friend why.**

A Mr Hall's favourite colour

B The day Mr Hall was sick

C Mr Hall's big mistake

❺ 💬 **Talk to four friends. Ask and answer the questions.**

1 Do you have red clothes?

2 Would you like a red bike? Why? / Why not?

3 What's your favourite colour?

4 How do you travel to school?

1 💬 **Look at the photos. Take turns to ask and answer: *What's the matter?***

TIP!

Remember: **ache** rhymes with **cake** and **cough** rhymes with **off**. Use *an* before words starting with *a, e, i, o, u*.

Ben

Paul

Vicky

Peter

Zoe

What's the matter with Ben?

He's got a cold.

2 🎧 29 **Listen. What does the doctor or nurse say the children must do? Complete the table. There is one example.**

Name	must ...
1 Ben	*drink water, eat vegetable soup*
2 Paul	
3 Vicky	
4 Peter	
5 Zoe	

3 **Check your answers with a friend.**

④ ✏️ **Imagine you are at the hospital. Use words from A, B and C to write two plays.**

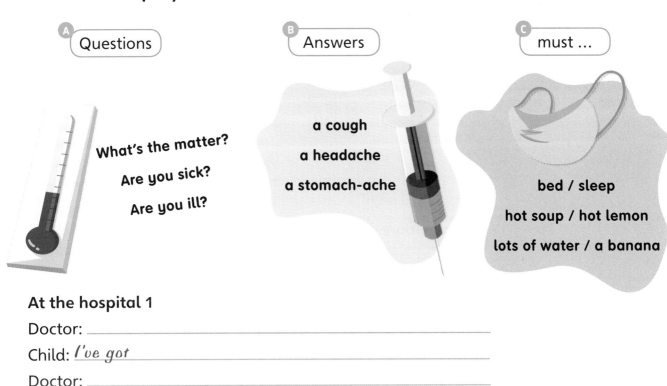

Ⓐ Questions

What's the matter?
Are you sick?
Are you ill?

Ⓑ Answers

a cough
a headache
a stomach-ache

Ⓒ must ...

bed / sleep
hot soup / hot lemon
lots of water / a banana

At the hospital 1

Doctor: _____

Child: *I've got* _____

Doctor: _____

At the hospital 2

Nurse: _____

Child: _____

Nurse: _____

⑤ 💬 **Practise your two plays with your friend. Take turns to be the doctor, the nurse and the child.**

⑥ **After you practise, show your class!**

THINK **BIG**

Are you healthy? Answer the questions with your friend:

1 Do you eat at least five fruit and vegetables a day? Which ones?

2 Do you play sport every week? Which sports?

Review Unit 9

Skills: Reading and Speaking

1 Work with a friend and choose four jobs each. Take turns to act (don't tell!) each job. Take turns and ask *what's my job?*

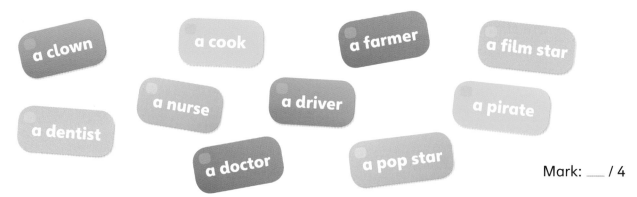

a clown   a cook   a farmer   a film star

a nurse   a driver   a pirate

a dentist   a doctor   a pop star

Mark: ___ / 4

2 Read about Dan's, Sally's and Vicky's dream jobs. Complete the sentences with their jobs. Copy the spellings carefully!

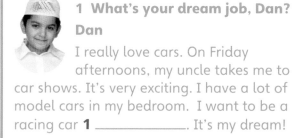

1 What's your dream job, Dan?
Dan
I really love cars. On Friday afternoons, my uncle takes me to car shows. It's very exciting. I have a lot of model cars in my bedroom. I want to be a racing car **1** _____. It's my dream!

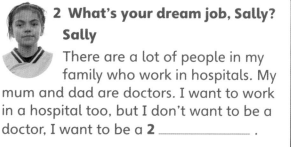

2 What's your dream job, Sally?
Sally
There are a lot of people in my family who work in hospitals. My mum and dad are doctors. I want to work in a hospital too, but I don't want to be a doctor, I want to be a **2** _____ .

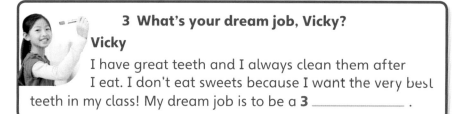

3 What's your dream job, Vicky?
Vicky
I have great teeth and I always clean them after I eat. I don't eat sweets because I want the very best teeth in my class! My dream job is to be a **3** _____ .

Mark: ___ / 3

3 Think about jobs you do at home. Which do you like LEAST?
Put them in order: 6 = I like this job LEAST!

go shopping
throw away rubbish
close the windows
clean the kitchen
tidy up toys
make my bed

1 _____
2 _____
3 _____
4 _____
5 _____
6 _____

Tell your friend why you like number 6 least!

Example: *I like to go shopping least because it's boring.*

Mark: ___ / 6

Total: ___ ___ / 13

Skills: Reading and Speaking

1 **Read Peter's story on page 50 again. Take turns to play *That's not true!* with a friend.**

> **A:** Peter loves cars.

> **B:** *That's not true! Peter loves paints!*

Mark: ___ / 3

2 **Change the words to make the sentences true.**

1 Peter got cars for his birthday.
2 He painted a picture for his mum.
3 He opened the paint in the classroom.
4 Peter went to school by train.
5 Mr Hall is Peter's doctor.
6 Peter had paint on his feet.
7 Peter was sick.
8 It was very sad.

Mark: ___ / 8

3 **Work with your friend and choose three illnesses each.**

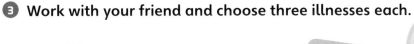

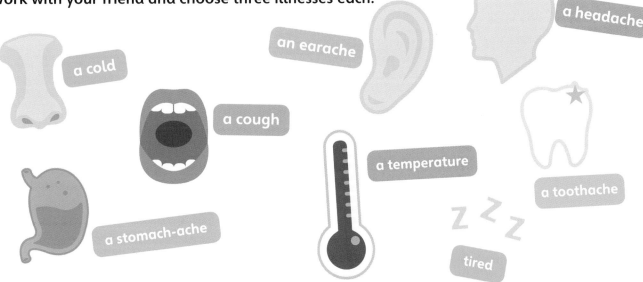

Show (don't tell!) your friend the illness.
Your friend asks *what's the matter?* Then says *I know! You've got a* _____ !
Say what they must do for each illness.

Mark: ___ / 3
Total: ___ / 14

> What's the matter?

> I know! You've got an earache!

> Hold a hot towel on your ear and go to bed.

1 🔊 **30** Look at picture 1. Listen and colour and write.

2 Look at picture 1 again. Close your book. What can you remember?

Here the river is blue.

Here the river is green.

3 💬 Pictures 1 and 2 look the same, but some colours are different. Talk to your partner. Tell your friend which colours are different.

4 💬 What other differences can you see?

Here the woman and the parrot are reading a book, and here they are ... .

5 👁 **Look at photos A and B and read the description. Which photo is it about?**

This photo is of an island. The sky is blue with white clouds in it. On the island there is a beach and there are some small buildings with brown roofs. There are some green trees on the island, too. In front of the island you can see a grey road. The sea around the island is blue. I like this photo because the island looks pretty and quiet and it's sunny. I would like to go swimming there.

6 **Read the description of the other island in 5 and fill in the gaps. You can use words from 5.**

This is a picture of an island. The sea **1** _____ the island is green and the sky is blue and **2** _____ .

3 _____ the island you can see a town. One of the buildings is very **4** _____ . There are some green trees on the **5** _____ too.

I like this photo because the island looks **6** _____ and **7** _____ .

I would like to visit the town there.

7 **Look at photo C and write. What would you like to do there? In pairs, look at the words you used, are they the same or different?**

1 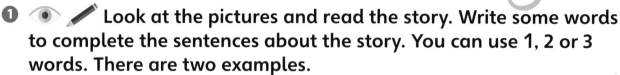 Look at the pictures and read the story. Write some words to complete the sentences about the story. You can use 1, 2 or 3 words. There are two examples.

Charlie's new home

Charlie lived in the countryside with his family. Their house was in a forest near a river, which made a lot of noise. And the birds sang every night – it wasn't quiet. But Charlie loved living there.

One day, Charlie's family moved to a flat in the city. It was next to a train station and the city was very different from the countryside. Charlie didn't like it. Every night trains went past his bedroom, so he couldn't sleep.

Charlie's house was in the _____*countryside*_____ .
It wasn't _____*quiet*_____ at night.

1 Charlie and his family went to live in a flat _____ .

2 Charlie's new home was near a _____ .

Charlie was tired when he went to school every day and he wasn't happy about this. He didn't know what to do.

Charlie's new friend Izzy wanted to help him. 'I have a good idea,' she said to Charlie on Monday. 'Let's go to the park after school,' said Izzy.

'OK,' answered Charlie.

3 Charlie wasn't happy at school because he was too _____ .

4 Izzy had a _____ to help Charlie.

5 Charlie was happy to go _____ after school.

Charlie and Izzy went to the park, and Izzy waved to a man who was near a tree. 'That's my dad,' said Izzy. 'And he has some roller skates for us.'

'Wow!' said Charlie. 'Can you teach me how to do roller skating?'
'Yes!' said Izzy. 'Come on!'

The next day, Charlie wasn't tired. 'I slept really well last night, Izzy. Can we go roller skating another day?'
'Yes!' laughed Izzy.

6 Izzy's dad brought _____ to the park for Izzy and Charlie.

7 Charlie wanted to go roller skating with Izzy _____ .

❷ 🔊31 **Listen and tick (✓) the correct sentences. There is one example.**

1 A Don't look at your computer or watch TV before you go to bed. ✓

   B It's better to look at your computer and watch lots of TV before you go to bed. ☐

2 A It's good to eat a big meal before you go to bed. ☐

   B Don't eat before you go to bed. ☐

3 A It's easier to sleep in a hot room. ☐

   B Try to sleep in a room that isn't too hot or too cold. ☐

4 A Do exercise in the day and you sleep better at night. ☐

   B Do exercise in the day and you sleep worse at night. ☐

❸ Talk to a friend about your sleep habits.

What time do you go to bed every day?

Is there something that helps you to sleep well? What is it?

(12) Watch a waterfall

1 👁 **Read Amal's list and choose the best title.**
A I want to watch a waterfall
B My favourite things
C Ten things I want to do this year

⭐ **5** _____
an animal from my hand.

⭐ **Build**
a brilliant
8 _____
with my brother.

⭐ **Read**
a **1** ___comic___
every day of the year.

⭐ **Learn**
to **3** _____,
because it's my dream.

⭐ **Run**
around in the
6 _____,
because it's fun.

⭐ **Find**
a box of
9 _____
in the park.

⭐ **Stand**
behind a
2 _____ and
watch the water fall.

⭐ **Climb**
a **4** _____
with my friends.

⭐ **7** _____
at ten o'clock every morning.

⭐ **10** _____
ten trees, because the world needs them!

2 **Now read Amal's list again and write the words.**

 comic

 sail

 feed

 rain

 treasure

 waterfall

 mountain

 snowman

 get up

 plant

❸ Read and colour the correct words.

I want to ice skate on a lake, [because] / [but] it's my dream.

1   I want to eat breakfast in bed [every] / [many] day.

2   I don't want to go to school, [because] / [with] it's boring.

3   I don't want to run around in the rain [and] / [because] it's cold.

4   I want to grow a tomato [and] / [because] eat it for dinner.

5   I want to build a tree house [because] / [with] my brother.

❹ ✏ Think about five things you want to do this year. Here are some ideas to start your list.

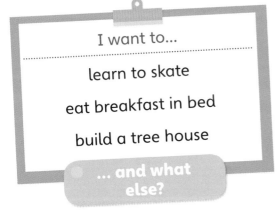

I want to...

learn to skate

eat breakfast in bed

build a tree house

... and what else?

because / every / with, etc.

because it's my dream

every day

with my brother

❺ Write your list.

I want to...

(1) _____

(2) _____

(3) _____

(4) _____

(5) _____

❻ 💬 Put your list with others from your group. Take one and guess who wrote it.

This person wants to learn to skate. I think it's Anna, because she loves sport.

❶ **Listen to the teacher's story. Point to the pictures.**

Dolly

Holly

❷ **Look at the missing words in task 3. Can you guess what they are?**

❸ 32 **Listen and write. There is one example.**

Going to the waterfall park.

Number of waterfalls at the park : ____*four*____

1 Name of biggest waterfall: _____ falls
2 Number of different kinds of parrots: _____
3 Can give food to: _____
4 Swimming pool next to: _____
5 Food in shop: _____

❹ **Read the riddle. Can you answer it?**

I am always running, but I don't have legs.
I make a loud noise, but I don't have a mouth.
I can be thin or fat, short or tall.
What am I?
I'm a _____ .

5 Read the song, look at the photos and write the animal words.

This pretty bird can talk.

It likes fresh fruit and carrots.

It's one of the cleverest birds in the world.

That's right! It's a _____ !

This cool animal is clever.

It eats cold fish and swims.

It never walks, it loves to play.

That's right! It's a _____ !

This little beast eats green leaves.

It's small and has no tail.

It's got a shell and two long eyes.

You guessed it! It's a _____ !

This fish is always hungry.

It's sometimes scary too.

It's got big teeth and it's very fast.

You guessed it! It's a _____ !

6 [33] Listen to the song and check your answers. Then sing the song.

7 ✏ Write an animal riddle and find a picture. Show your friends.
Can you guess their riddles?

Skills: Writing and Speaking

1 Draw and colour a picture of your favourite place. Choose a place that's outside, not inside. Make sure you draw everything that you can see in that place.

> the weather   plants   building   animals   sea / lake / river

Now make notes in the column in the table about your favourite place.
When there isn't an answer – you can write 'There aren't any.'

Questions	My favourite place	_____'s favourite place
1 What's your favourite place? e.g. My grandma's house.		
2 Where is it?		
3 What's the weather like in the picture?		
4 Are there plants? What are they?		
5 Are there buildings? What are they?		
6 Is there water? What is it?		
7 Are there animals? What are they?		
8 Why do you like it?		

2 Ask and answer with your friend. Fill in the table with their answers.

> What's your favourite place?

> It's my grandma's house.

Total: ___ ___ / 16

Skills: Listening and Reading

1 34 **Listen to Aria talk about things that she wants to do and number the pictures in order. There is one example.**

Mark: ___ / 5

2 35 **Listen to Aria again and check your answers.**

3 **What's wrong? Read and think. Can you correct the red phrases so that they are correct?**

This year, Aria wants to do six new things. First, she wants to climb the tree in the park and have

a picnic lunch

1) ~~chocolate ice-cream~~ up there. Second, she wants to build a house for the ducks because she

thinks that they have **2)** a hot shower at night. Then, Aria wants to learn to make **3)** a picnic lunch

for her friends. After that, she wants to look for the treasure. Her sister says that it's in **4)** the sea.

Next, Aria wants to swim with dolphins because they love to play in **5)** the forest. Last of all, Aria

wants to get really wet and then she wants to have **6)** cold feet.

Mark: ___ / 5

Total: ___ ___ / 10

Songs and chants

Unit 1, page 7
Hey Lily!

Student A:	Hey Lily!
Lily:	Hey you!
Student A:	What can we do in Kota Kinabalu?
Lily:	We can watch elephants through my telescope!
Student A:	Is that true?
Student B:	Hey Lily!
Lily:	Hey you!
Student B:	What can we do in Kota Kinabalu?
Lily:	We can go shopping and roller skating too!
Student B:	Is that true?
Student A:	Hey Lily!
Lily:	Hey you!
Student A:	What can we do in Kota Kinabalu?
Lily:	We can drink milkshakes with Charlie the bat!
Student A:	Is that true?
Lily and Student A and Student B:	Yes, it's true!!!

Unit 2, page 12
Our amazing pets

Claire:	My pet rabbit's called Daisy.
Claire:	It likes pancakes and picnics!
Jim:	My pet puppy's called Zoe.
Jim:	It loves swimming in our garden pool!
Jane:	My pet parrot's called Paul.
Jane:	It goes skating on the big lake!
Ali:	My pet kitten's called Ahmad.
Ali:	It dresses up in funny ties!

Unit 3, page 16

About town

I parked in the car park in my small, red car,
Then I went to the hospital to see my sick grandma,
Then I bought a bag of apples in the market square
And last of all I met my friends at the big funfair!

I arrived at the station on a new orange train,
Then I went to the cinema to watch a film called Rain.
Then I went to the New Café to drink a cup of tea
And last of all I read some comics in the library.

Songs and chants

Unit 5, page 28
My dream school

Girl 1: My dream school is really brilliant!
Our classroom is in a cinema.
We use e-books to learn English.
It's like you are on Mars!!

Boy 1: My dream school is in the jungle.
There's always lots to see and do.
We are pirates who look for treasure.
Our classroom really is the best.

Boy 2: My dream school is so fantastic!
Our classroom is in a cool café.
We drink milkshakes and wear baseball caps.
Visit my dream school today!

Girl 2: My dream school is like a wonderland.
Our teachers here are all great fun.
We read comics and we sing English songs.
Come inside and have a look around
my dream school.

Unit 6, page 31
Food

Apple pie, apple pie
Burger and chips, burger and chips
Cheese sandwich, cheese sandwich
Chocolate ice cream, chocolate ice cream
Orange juice, orange juice!

Unit 12, page 63
Animals

This pretty bird can talk.
It likes fresh fruit and carrots,
It's one of the cleverest birds in the world.
That's right! It's a parrot!

This cool animal is clever,
It eats cold fish and swims,
It never walks, it loves to play!
That's right! It's a dolphin!

This little beast eats green leaves,
It's small and has no tail.
It's got a shell and two long eyes.
You guessed it! It's a snail!

This fish is always hungry.
It's sometimes scary too!
It's got big teeth and it's very fast.
You guessed it! It's a shark!

Unit 1

·····O *When* clauses

I can hear the waterfall at night **when** I'm in bed.
When the teacher talked, we listened.

1 Match the two parts of the sentence.

1 When I go to bed,   A when it's cold.

2 I put on my coat   B I dream.

3 I hurt my leg   C when I fell from a tree.

4 When I go to sleep,   D I get undressed.

2 Correct the sentences. Rewrite them with *when*.

1 he got home, he had his lunch.

_____

2 I jumped she shouted.

_____

3 they see funny clowns, they laugh.

_____

4 we go to bed we're tired.

_____

Unit 2

·····O Prepositions of time

Daisy goes for a picnic **on** Monday mornings.
She cleans her teeth **at** 12 o'clock.
She plays with her friends **after** school.
She has breakfast **before** school.

1 Choose the correct words.

1 Let's meet **on** / **at** 3 o'clock.

2 Wash your hands **on** / **before** dinner.

3 Hugo goes shopping **after** / **on** Saturdays.

4 **At** / **Before** lunch, I went ice skating.

5 I did my homework in the morning **after** / **before** school.

6 My mum was tired **on** / **after** work.

2 Complete the conversation with *on*, *at*, *after* or *before*.

Julia: Jim, what did you do (1) _____ school yesterday evening?

Jim: First, I went roller skating. (2) _____ roller skating, I had dinner and went to bed (3) _____ 9 o'clock. And you?

Julia: I had lots of homework to do (4) _____ today, so I went home (5) _____ school. Our teacher always gives us lots of homework (6) _____ Thursdays.

Grammar fun!

Unit 3

⊙ *Go + -ing*

> I **go swimming** on Saturdays.
> We **went shopping** yesterday.

1 Look and complete the sentences. Use the correct form of *go* and these words.

> fishing   skateboarding   riding   ice skating
> roller skating

 Cristina
 Arda
 Emma

 Francesca and Hugo
 Peter and Zoe

1 Cristina —————— last week.

2 Arda always —————— at the weekend.

3 Emma —————— every morning.

4 Francesca and Hugo —————— yesterday.

5 Peter and Zoe —————— last Monday.

⊙ Infinitive of purpose

> Dan went to the pet shop **to buy a puppy**.

2 Match the two parts of the sentence.

1 I go to bed   A to say hello.

2 I dressed up   B to sleep.

3 I phoned Charlie   C to go to the party.

4 I clean my   D to help my
  bedroom   parents.

3 Complete the sentences with the correct forms of these verbs.

> invite   buy   score   go

1 Anna went to town —————— a new T-shirt.

2 Mary gets up at 7 o'clock —————— to school.

3 Robert texted Paolo —————— him to a party.

4 Jane kicked the ball —————— a goal.

Unit 4

⊙ Adverbs of frequency

> Jack **never** falls.
> He **always** laughs.
> He **often** dresses up.
> He dances **sometimes**. / He **sometimes** dances. / **Sometimes**, he dances.

1 Write the adverbs.

4 ——————

3 ——————

2 ——————

1 *never*

2 Rewrite the sentences using the adverbs.

1 Zoe eats meat. (never)

——————————————————————.

2 Vicky rides a bike. (often)

——————————————————————.

3 Peter's dog is hungry. (always)

——————————————————————.

4 Julio's horse is naughty. (sometimes)

——————————————————————.

Unit 5

⊙ *Be good at + noun*

> What are you **good at**?
> **Is he good at** singing?
> I**'m good at** English.
> Daisy**'s not good at** basketball.
> Paul and Charlie **aren't good at** colouring.

> 'm = am   's = is

1 Put the words in the correct order.

1 good / are / drawing? / at / you

_____

2 mum's / at / fishing. / my / good

_____

3 at? / good / Fred / what's

_____

4 roller skating. / not / he's / at / good

_____

2 Complete the sentences about the pictures. Use *good at* (✓) or *not good at* (✗) and these words.

> music   ice skating   football   tennis

Peter

_____. (✓)

Mary

_____. (✗)

Unit 6

⊙ *I think/know …*

> **I think our teacher's** very nice.
> **I don't think Charlie can** drive.
> **I thought it was** funny.

> **I know** his name.
> **I don't know** where he lives.
> When the teacher asked the question,
> **I knew** the answer.

1 Complete the sentences with the correct form of *know* or *think*.

1 Matt _____ he's good at skating, but he isn't.

2 I _____ Jack's number, so I couldn't call him.

3 Zoe _____ you're here because she can see you from her window.

4 My friend _____ it was my birthday yesterday. But my birthday is today!

5 They _____ it was a dolphin, but it was a whale.

Zoe and Julia

_____. (✓)

Jack and Jim

_____. (✗)

Grammar fun!

Unit 7

○ Verb + infinitive

> What would Sarah **like to do** today?
> Hugo **started to laugh**.

1 Complete the sentences. Use the infinitive of these verbs.

ride   hurt   get up   send   play   ~~go~~

1 Jim wants some new roller skates. He needs ____*to go*____ shopping.

2 My grandma likes _____ at 5 in the morning.

3 Alice tried _____ a photo, but the internet was too slow.

4 Ben is learning _____ a bike. His sister teaches him every day.

5 At school, Jane chose _____ the guitar, not the piano.

6 I'm sorry! I didn't mean _____ you.

○ How / what about + noun or -ing

> **How/What about going** for an ice cream?
> **How/What about an ice cream**?

2 Complete the sentences. Use these nouns.

this DVD   a parrot   a pancake

1 A: I'm hungry.
   B: How about _____ ?

2 A: This film's boring.
   B: What about _____ ?

3 A: I'd like a pet.
   B: How about _____ ?

3 Complete the sentences. Use these verbs in the *ing* form.

buy   go   cook

1 A: I'm hungry.
   B: What about _____ some pasta?

2 A: This film's boring.
   B: How / What about _____ to the park?

3 A: I'd like a pet.
   B: What about _____ a rabbit?

Unit 8

○ Question words *why, when, where, how*

> **Why** did you go there?
> **When** did it happen?
> **Where** did you go?
> **How** did it end?

1 Match the questions and answers.

1 Why is Sally talking to Kim?
2 When does school start?
3 Where are Mustafa and Miguel?
4 How did you break it?

A At 9 o'clock.
B In the playground.
C I dropped it.
D To practise Spanish.

2 Put the questions in the correct order.

1 where / shopping? / go / you / did
   _____

2 did / Daisy / hurt / foot? / her / how
   _____

3 football? / you / play / do/ when
   _____

4 Jack / silly / hat? / why / wearing / a / is
   _____

Unit 9

···O   Superlative adverbs

good/well
What do you like **best** about your school?
badly
Everyone sang badly, but Jack sang the **worst**.
slowly, quickly, etc.
Who ran **most** slow**ly**?
Eva ran **most** quick**ly**.
Hugo speaks **most** loud**ly**.
Fred speaks **most** quiet**ly**.

1 Complete the sentences with the superlative adverb.

1 Sally climbed the mountain ———— .
   (quickly)

2 Jackie sings ———— in our class.
   (loudly)

3 Ed's good at ice skating, but Clare skates
   ———— . (well)

4 Who do you think draws ———— at
   school? (badly)

5 My uncle drives ———— in my family.
   (slowly)

6 I like lots of food, but I like ice cream
   ———— . (good)

Unit 10

···O   Adverbs of degree

We laughed **a lot**.
The room was **very** cold.

1 Put the sentences in the correct order.

1 weekends. / a lot / sleeps / at / Julia

   ————————————————————

2 sky / is / today. / very / grey / the

   ————————————————————

3 a lot / dance / you / did / at / party? / the

   ————————————————————

4 very / was / yesterday. / tired / Dan

   ————————————————————

2 Write the sentences with *a lot* or *very* in the correct position.

1 My mother talks.

   ———————————————————— .

2 She's good at tennis.

   ———————————————————— .

3 My drink wasn't cold.

   ———————————————————— .

4 His baby sister grew last year.

   ———————————————————— .

Grammar fun!

Unit 11

○ *Must* for obligation

> He **must** do his homework.
> Your room **mustn't** be too hot or too cold.
> **Must** I feed the cat?

> mustn't = must not

1 Match the two parts of the sentence .

1 You mustn't talk   A quiet when the teacher talks.

2 Must I   B get up now?

3 We must be   C to school by 8:30.

4 We must come   D loudly in a hospital.

2 Complete the sentences with *must* and one of the verbs in the box.

be   drive   dress up   bounce   wear   clean

1 You ————— your teeth before you go to bed.

2 People ————— slowly near our school.

3 Boys ————— trousers at our school, not shorts.

4 We ————— to go to the party.

5 When you play basketball, you ————— the ball.

6 When you go roller skating, you ————— careful.

Unit 12

○ Indirect objects

> Give your homework to **the teacher**.
> Dad gave it to **me**.

1 Put the sentences in the correct order.

1 drawing / Lily / me. / gave / her / to

_____

2 gave / teddy / Jack / the / Molly. / to

_____

3 to / Jim / rollers skates / his / her. / gave

_____

4 milkshake / gave / Clare / Ben. / her / to

_____

2 Look and write sentences.

1 _____. (sent)

2 _____. (gave)

3 _____. (gave)

Unit 1

⋯○ *When* clauses

1 Complete the sentences and ask a friend.

When I'm happy, I smile. And you?
When I'm happy, I sing!

When I'm happy ...   ... I eat some food.
When I'm sad ...   ... I play a game.
When I'm tired ...   ... I laugh.

Unit 3

⋯○ Go + *ing*

2 Make questions with *Do you like going* and these words. Talk with a friend.

shopping   roller skating   riding   fishing
dancing   swimming

Do you like going shopping?

Yes, I do.

When do you go shopping?

I go shopping at weekends.

Unit 8

Student A

⋯○ Question words *why, when, where, how*

3 Complete the sentences. Student B has the information you need. Ask and answer questions.

Student B: look at page 77.

A: *Where did Jack go?*
B: *He went to _the circus_ .*

Jack went to ———— (where?)
on ———— (when?). He went by
———— (how?).

Julia travels to school by train because she lives in a different city.

On ———— (when?), Emma went shopping to ———— (why?). The party is at ———— (where?).

Charlie plays football after school on Thursdays. He goes home in his mum's car.

Unit 4

Student A

⋯○ Adverbs of frequency

4 Complete the table. Student B has the information you need. Ask *How often ...?* Write *never*, *sometimes*, *often* or *always*. Answer your friend's questions.

Student B: look at page 77.

A: *How often does Bolt listen to music?*
B: *He _sometimes_ listens to music.*

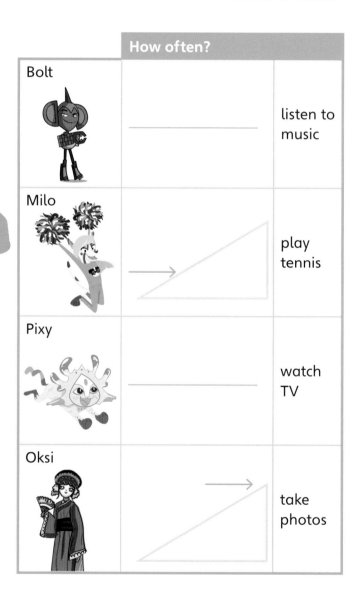

	How often?	
Bolt	————	listen to music
Milo	→	play tennis
Pixy	————	watch TV
Oksi	→	take photos

Grammar fun pairwork!

Unit 3

O Infinitive of purpose

5 **Complete the sentences with a friend. Check with the class. Who wrote most answers?**

> *We go to school to learn, to have fun, to play ...*

We go to school to ...
I went shopping to ...
I phoned my friend to ...
She waved to ...
He made a cake to ...
I got up at 5 am to ...

Unit 8

Student B

O Question words *why*, *when*, *where*, *how*

6 **Complete the sentences. Student A has the information you need. Ask and answer questions.**

Student A: look at page 76.

> **A:** *Where did Jack go?*
> **B:** *He went to* ___the circus___ .

Jack went to the circus on Sunday. He went by bus.

Julia travels to _____ *(where?)*
by _____ *(how?) because she*
_____ *(why?).*

On Saturday, Emma went shopping to buy a birthday present. The party is at her cousin's house.

Charlie plays _____ *(what?)*
_____ *(when?). He goes home*
_____ *(how?).*

Unit 4

Student B

O Adverbs of frequency

7 **Complete the table. Student A has the information you need. Ask *How often ...?* Write *never*, *sometimes*, *often* or *always*. Answer your friend's questions.**

Student A: look at page 76.

> **A:** *How often does Bolt listen to music?*
> **B:** *He* ___sometimes___ *listens to music.*

	How often?	
Bolt	→	listen to music
Milo	_____	play tennis
Pixy	→	watch TV
Oksi	_____	take photos

Reading & Writing Checklist

Circle  if your answer is Yes!

I am good at spelling words and copying them.

I know and can spell all seven days of the week.

I enjoy looking at pictures and answering questions about them.

I like matching pictures to the correct part of a story.

I can read and understand short stories with pictures.

I like reading stories in English in class.

I can write short sentences about a picture.

I know and can spell ten words for things in school.

It's fun to finish a story by filling in gaps.

I can write two sentences about my routines.

I can write three sentences about my town in task 6 on page 17.

How many magic squirrels did you get?

Reading & Writing Checklist

Check your progress, colour the stars!

	OK	Great

I can write a play and act it out.

I can match words for things in a town to the correct pictures.

I had lots of good ideas and great words to describe my dream school on page 29.

I know and can spell some weather words on page 36.

I can fill in the story on page 50 with the correct words.

I chose the best title for the story on page 50.

I can describe where things are using the words in task 5 on page 57.

I understand and can solve the riddle on page 62.

I enjoyed reading the stories in the book.

Listening Checklist

Circle  if your answer is Yes!

I can understand a lot when my teacher speaks English.

I am good at writing words when I hear the spelling.

I was able to match the correct pictures to Lily's description of her routine in task 3 on page 14.

I drew a good picture of what Vicky and her friends ate after listening to the story in task 2 on page 18.

I know and can spell ten words for things in school.

I know when to spell, write or tick in the listening tasks.

I filled in the gaps in the song with the correct words in task 1 on page 28.

I enjoyed matching the right names to the pictures in task 1 on page 46.

I know which picture to choose when I hear a description.

I can write two sentences about my routines.

I filled in the correct information in the gaps in task 3 on page 62.

I know the colours and like colouring the picture when I listen to the description.

How many magic squirrels did you get?

Speaking Checklist

Check your progress, colour the stars!

	OK	Great
I can tell people about myself in English.	☆	☆☆
I interviewed four friends about what they do and guessed their false answers in tasks 3 and 4 on page 9.	☆	☆☆
I can ask people to repeat a question if I don't understand what they said.	☆	☆☆
I described a place clearly so my friend could guess where it was in task 2 on page 24.	☆	☆☆
I can use lots of adjectives to describe pictures.	☆	☆☆
I talked about my favourite food with my friend in task 4 on page 31.	☆	☆☆
I talked about what I did last weekend in task 6 and 7 on page 41.	☆	☆☆
I have lots of good ideas for telling a story.	☆	☆☆
I asked and answered questions about classroom jobs in task 3 on page 49.	☆	☆☆
I am good at answering questions with more than one or two words, because it is fun to talk in English.	☆	☆☆

Word list

Unit 1

afraid *adj* _____

balcony *n* _____

bat *n* _____

buy *v* _____

farm *n* _____

grandparent *n* _____

jungle *n* _____

milkshake *n* _____

parrot *n* _____

roller skating *n* _____

shopping centre *n* _____

village *n* _____

waterfall *n* _____

Unit 2

band (music) *n* _____

dance *n+v* _____

dolphin *n* _____

fat *adj* _____

ice skating *n* _____

kangaroo *n* _____

laugh *v* _____

pancake *n* _____

penguin *n* _____

picnic *n* _____

rabbit *n* _____

shark *n* _____

snail *n* _____

supermarket *n* _____

whale *n* _____

Unit 3

café *n* _____

car park *n* _____

cheese *n* _____

cinema *n* _____

comic *n* _____

cup *n* _____

film *n* _____

funfair *n* _____

hospital *n* _____

lake *n* _____

library *n* _____

map *n* _____

market *n* _____

park *n* _____

puppy *n* _____

rain *n+v* _____

sandwich *n* _____

sick *adj* _____

square *n* _____

star *n* _____

station *n* _____

tea *n* _____

train *n* _____

Unit 4

baseball *n* _____

basketball *n* _____

countryside *n* _____

dance *v* _____

farmer *n* _____

field *n* _____

grass *n* _____

kick *n* _____

mountain *n* _____

sail *n+v* _____

skates *n* _____

sport *n* _____

tennis *adj* _____

Unit 5

boring *adj* _____

circus *n* _____

clown *n* _____

dream *n+v* _____

e-book *n* _____

pirate *n* _____

teach *v* _____

treasure *n* _____

Unit 6

burger *n* _____

city *n* _____

cook *v* _____

fish *n* _____

fruit *n* _____

noodles *n* _____

pasta *n* _____

pizza *n* _____

salad *n* _____

sauce *n* _____

soup *n* _____

Unit 7

cloudy *adj* _____

cold *adj* _____

DVD *n* _____

fall *v* _____

hot *adj* _____

ice *n* _____

snow *n+v* _____

weather *n* _____

wet *adj* _____

wind *n* _____

windy *adj* _____

Unit 8

climb *v* _____

dangerous *adj* _____

scarf *n* _____

tired *adj* _____

wake (up) *v* _____

Unit 9

carry *v* _____

coat *n* _____

dentist *n* _____

dress up *v* _____

film star *n* _____

nurse *n* _____

party *n* _____

pop star *n* _____

tractor *n* _____

vegetable *n* _____

window *n* _____

Unit 10

cough *n* _____

earache *n* _____

fine *adj* _____

headache *n* _____

paint *n* _____

panda *n* _____

stomach-ache *n* _____

temperature *n* _____

toothache *n* _____

Unit 11

asleep *adj* _____

flat *n* _____

forest *n* _____

kitten *n* _____

leaf / leaves *n* _____

loud *adj* _____

roof *n* _____

wave *v* _____

Unit 12

grow *v* _____

plant *n+v* _____

swimsuit *n* _____

tooth / teeth *n* _____

In your book ...

Bolt

Likes: sleeping on the beach, running in the forest, flying in the air

Dislikes: octopuses, sleeping in a cave

Milo

Likes: pizza, running, playing football, treats

Dislikes: flying, singing, pancakes

Oksi

Likes: singing, dancing, flying, fans

Dislikes: watching TV, meat, dogs

Woody

Likes: flying very high, fruit

Dislikes: swimming in the sea, vegetables

Skippy

Likes: meat, skipping

Dislikes: watching TV, going to school

Pixy

Likes: fresh fish, water, plants

Dislikes: noise, light

... from kids around the world

Judy, 8

Mariyam, 10

Nikita, 9

Alejandro, 10

Vaja, 9

Daniel, 9

Checklist buddy

Likes: pizza, apple juice, playing ball

Dislikes: ice cream, burgers, mice, cats

Exam Professor

Likes: science, music, interesting animals, playing basketball

Dislikes: disorder, meat, destruction, black

Think Big Giraffe

Likes: plants

Dislikes: meat

Sage

Likes: reading, eating, joking, art

Dislikes: pickles, flies, the dark, cockroaches

Mariya, 8

Mario, 11

Adriana, 7

Edith, 11

Author acknowledgements

Bridget Kelly would like to thank Ann-Marie, Lynn and David - she really enjoyed working with them all. And thanks to Colin and little Aedan as always.

David Valente would like to sincerely thank Katherine Bilsborough and Emily Hird for being great sounding boards throughout the writing process.

Publisher acknowledgements

The authors and publishers are grateful to the following for reviewing the material during the writing process:

Lucie Cotterill, Jane Ritter, Khara Burgess: Italy; Muruvvet Celik: Turkey; Nguyen Hoa, Georges Erhard: Vietnam; Roisin O'Farrell: Spain; Gustavo Baron Sanchez: Mexico.

The authors and publishers acknowledge the following sources of copyright material and are grateful for the permissions granted. While every effort has been made, it has not always been possible to identify the sources of all the material used, or to trace all copyright holders. If any omissions are brought to our notice, we will be happy to include the appropriate acknowledgements on reprinting & in the next update to the digital edition, as applicable.

Key: Gr: Grammar; U: Unit.

Photography

The following photographs are sourced from Getty Images.
Gr: Adie Bush/Image Source; dimid_86/iStock/Getty Images Plus; Glow Images, Inc; MamiEva/RooM; UpperCut Images; **U1:** Morsa Images/DigitalVision; Fabio Lamanna/EyeEm; Westend61; RichVintage/E+; Punnawit Suwuttananun/Moment; andresr/E+; Emilija Manevska/Moment; Slawomir Tomas/EyeEm; yusnizam/iStock/Getty Images Plus; robas/E+; Cherry Tantirathanon/EyeEm; NurPhoto; Daniel Limpi/EyeEm; Avalon/Universal Images Group; **U2:** Fadi Mckean/EyeEm; Karina Mansfield/Moment; EMS-FORSTER-PRODUCTIONS/DigitalVision; Westend61; Sean_Warren/E+; 2A Images; JGI/Jamie Grill; **U3:** SensorSpot/E+; GSO Images/Photodisc; Flashpop/DigitalVision; AFP; Hufton and Crow/Corbis Documentary; Stephen Dorey/Photolibrary; Dave Shafer/Aurora; Tom Sibley/Corbis; Nikada/iStock Unreleased; Eakachai Leesin/EyeEm; drbimages/iStock/Getty Images Plus; **U4:** Jose Luis Pelaez Inc/DigitalVision; Ty Allison/Taxi; Tony Garcia/Image Source; Shoji Fujita/DigitalVision; Mark Hunt; Jupiterimages/Polka Dot/Getty Images Plus; Seb Oliver/Cultura; Compassionate Eye Foundation/Natasha Alipour Faridani/DigitalVision; LifeJourneys/E+; photography by Linda Lyon/Moment; Matthew Ashmore/EyeEm; **U5:** andresr/E+; kali9/E+; Tim Hall/Cultura; Hill Street Studios/DigitalVision; PhotoAlto/Sigrid Olsson; xavierarnau/E+; Alexei Polyansky/EyeEm; Sue Barr/Image Source; **U6:** Maskot; Erick Olvera/EyeEm; Westend61; Indeed; Thiti Sukapan/EyeEm; hadynyah/E+; Massimo Lama/EyeEm; Martin Deja/Moment; Slawomir Tomas/EyeEm; Elizabeth Livermore/Moment; hdere/E+; vinicef/iStock/Getty Images Plus; IngaNielsen/iStock/Getty Images Plus; Steve Lewis Stock/Photographer's Choice; Jose Luis Pelaez Inc/DigitalVision; Nancy Honey/Cultura; Andersen Ross/Stockbyte; Monkey Business Images; FuatKose/E+; real444/E+; CactuSoup/iStock/Getty Images Plus; CactuSoup/E+; JLPH/Cultura; twomeows/Moment; paul mansfield photography/Moment; Luis Alvarez/DigitalVision; Alexei Polyansky/EyeEm; David Sacks/The Image Bank; Jasmin Merdan/Moment; Science Photo Library; **U7:** Per Eriksson; Arata Ishida/EyeEm; **U8:** Andreas Ulvdell/Folio Images; jreika/iStock/Getty Images Plus; Giovanna Graf/EyeEm; Aliraza Khatri's Photography/Moment; Bob Peterson/UpperCut Images; Gerard Puigmal/Moment; amenic181/iStock/Getty Images Plus; Louis Turner/Cultura; Jeff Titcomb/Stone; PeopleImages/E+; Artyom Geodakyan/TASS; Godong/Universal Images Group; Esther Moreno Martinez/EyeEm; Emma Kim/Cultura; **U9:** Compassionate Eye Foundation/DigitalVision; photosindia; Hero Images; Inti St Clair/DigitalVision; **U10:** Hero Images; BananaStock; kwanchaichaiudom/iStock/Getty Images Plus; 1MoreCreative/iStock/Getty Images Plus; Ismailciydem/iStock/Getty Images Plus; Sawitree Pamee/EyeEm; **U11:** Christian Offenberg/EyeEm; Michele Falzone/AWL Images; Rafal Nycz/Moment; FG Trade/iStock/Getty Images Plus; **U12:** Christophe Bourloton/iStock/Getty Images Plus; MakiEni's photo/Moment; John Russell/EyeEm; Will Heap/Dorling Kindersley; Ramn Carretero/EyeEm; Shutter Chemistry/500px Prime; Shutter Chemistry/500px Prime.

The following photograph is sourced from other library.
U4: MARK HICKEN/Alamy Stock Photo.

Front cover photography by Amanda Enright; Jhonny Nunez; Leo Trinidad; Pol Cunyat; Dan Widdowson; Pipi Sposito; Pand P Studio/Shutterstock; Piotr Urakau/Shutterstock

Illustrations

Amanda Enright (Advocate); Leo Trinidad (Bright); Fran Brylewska (Beehive); Pipi Sposito (Advocate); Pablo Gallego (Beehive); Dave Williams (Bright); Collaborate Agency; Wild Apple Design Ltd

Front cover illustrations by Amanda Enright; Jhonny Nunez; Leo Trinidad; Pol Cunyat; Dan Widdowson; Pipi Sposito; Pand P Studio/Shutterstock; Piotr Urakau/Shutterstock

Audio

Audio production by Ian Harker

Songs composition, vocals and production by Robert Lee at Dib Dib Dub Studios, UK.

Chants composition and production by AmyJo Doherty and Martin Spangle.

Design

Design and typeset by Wild Apple Design Ltd
Cover design by Collaborate agency